KU-345-435

HENRY V

By Jennifer Mulherin   Illustrations by Patricia Ludlow
CHERRYTREE BOOKS

Author's note

There is no substitute for seeing the plays of Shakespeare performed. Only then can you really understand why Shakespeare is our greatest dramatist and poet. This book gives you the background to the play and tells you about the story and characters – and a taste of Shakespeare's language. It will, I hope, encourage you to see the play.

A Cherrytree Book

Designed and produced by
A S Publishing

First published 2001
by Cherrytree Press
327 High Street
Slough
Berkshire
SL1 1TX

© Evans Brothers Limited 2001

British Library Cataloguing in Publication Data

Mulherin, Jennifer
    Henry V – (Shakespeare For Everyone)
    I. Shakespeare, William, 1564-1616. Henry V – Juvenile literature
    2. Shakespeare, William, 1564-1616. – Adaptations – Juvenile literature
    I. Title II.
    822.3'3

ISBN 1 84234 031 X (hardcover)
ISBN 1 84234 050 6 (softcover)

Printed in Hong Kong through Colorcraft Ltd.

Contents

Defeating England's enemies

Physical descriptions of the young Henry V mention his strong and athletic build and his good looks, features that are captured in this portrait of him by Benjamin Burnell (1769-1828).

Shakespeare's *Henry V* tells the story of how a heroic English king and his army defeated the country's traditional enemy, France. This was a subject dear to the Elizabethans. Inspired by their queen, Elizabeth I, they too had vanquished powerful enemies.

England's enemies

Elizabeth ruled England as a Protestant monarch, opposed by Catholic Rome, France and Spain. At the time, Spain was the most powerful country in Europe. Its king, Philip II, was alarmed by the strength and unity that Elizabeth I had brought to her country. Despite rebellions in Ireland and religious strife at home, there was peace and prosperity in England. Adventurous seafarers sailed to the New World, and English pirates even dared to make attacks on the Spanish fleet. Philip decided to act. In May 1588, he sent a huge fleet of ships to attack the Kent coast and march on London.

The Spanish Armada

The English knew of the Spanish plans and were prepared. Beacons set up along the coast warned of the Armada's approach. The fleets were evenly matched. The Spanish had more ships and men but the English had more cannon. Despite some daring manoeuvres by the English captains, bad weather prevented the navy from doing serious damage to the Spanish fleet. The Armada kept its formation and moved slowly up the English Channel to Calais.

Fire at night

On the night of 28 July, the English set alight eight ships laden with pitch and gunpowder, and let them drift towards the Spanish fleet. The Armada captains panicked. None of their ships caught fire, but the Armada broke its formations and headed for the North Sea in disarray. There, English ships attacked the galleons one by one, forcing them into treacherous waters off Scotland and Ireland. The battle was lost. Of the 138 Armada ships, only 67 returned to Spain.

English and Spanish ships exchange cannon fire in this depiction of the sea battle of July 1588, painted around 1600 by Hendrik Cornelisz Vroom.

This glorious victory was still fresh in the minds of the English when Shakespeare wrote *Henry V* in 1599. People could see parallels between the story of the Battle of Agincourt and their recent triumph. The famous battle of 1415 was a high point in English history. Every Elizabethan citizen knew about it and of the country's great king Henry V.

Battle of Agincourt

At Agincourt, the English troops were outnumbered by the French. Again, it was because of English daring, skill – and bad weather – that the battle was won. Weighed down by heavy armour, the French advanced across water-logged fields. They became stuck in the mud, and were easy prey for the English archers.

Henry had made his archers move to within bowshot

range. This was a risky move, which paid off – his men could have been attacked by French cavalry before they were in position. It took great strength and practice to use the longbow, which was as tall as a man. A skilled archer could fire about 12 arrows per minute.

The Elizabethans knew that courage and optimism often win against the odds. History had told them so, and Shakespeare reminded them of it in *Henry V*. With these qualities and a great leader, England had – and would in the future – overcome her enemies.

Right: This painting, dated 1996, of King Henry addressing his troops on St Crispian's Day, is by the modern British artist Philip Sutton.

The ideal king?

Shakespeare's audience was already familiar with the character of Henry V. He appears in two previous history plays of Shakespeare – *Henry IV Part 1* and *Henry IV Part 2*. In the first play, Henry is a disappointment to the king, his father. He is more interested in merrymaking than in the court or the business of government. He spends his

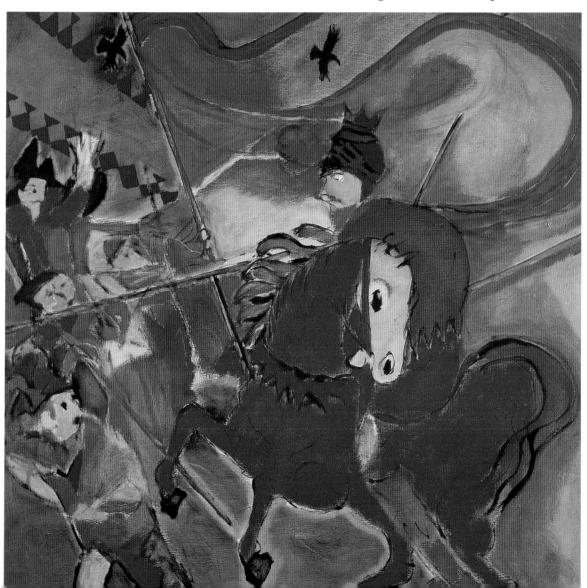

time in taverns with disreputable characters like Sir John Falstaff, who was renowned for excess in all things.

In the second play, Prince Hal (Henry) is reconciled with his father. He distances himself from his old cronies. He knows he must assume the responsibilities of a king. When his father dies and he becomes king, he publicly rejects Falstaff.

A modern play

In this way, Shakespeare prepares us for the Henry V of the play. He has become a wise and noble ruler. He is also a popular one because of his experience of life among the common people. Like all Elizabethans, Shakespeare greatly admired the historical Henry V. He is his favourite hero in English history, and we feel Shakespeare meant to portray him as the ideal ruler. But Henry is also a very human figure, who is not always sure he is doing the right thing. This is what makes him interesting, and is one reason why the play is still appreciated by people today.

Shakespeare presents Henry and the whole business of war from many different angles. In modern times, as in Shakespeare's day, we are concerned about the rights and wrongs of war. Shakespeare does not glorify war, but it is sometimes necessary, he suggests, to defend one's country. When that happens, we should show patriotism.

Patriotism in times of war

Most people see *Henry V* as a patriotic play. Indeed, it celebrates a great victory. In times of war, it has certainly rallied and inspired people to do their utmost for their country. The best-known version of the play is Laurence Olivier's spectacular film of 1944, made during World War II. After five years of war, the film was intended to

The exhaustion of the English soldiers on the morning of Agincourt is captured in this painting by Sir John Gilbert (1817-97).

boost the morale of the exhausted British soldiers and civilians. It did so with dazzling success.

In 1944, the British army had to cross the English Channel on D-Day to fight a dangerous and powerful enemy. It would land in France close to where Henry's

soldiers had fought some 600 years before. One soldier –
a Yorkshire captain – repeated to his men Henry V's
words before Agincourt. He died heroically in action.

Henry V had also matched the mood of the time in
1914, when World War I broke out. One critic, who had
always thought of the play as 'perfunctory', changed his
view of it. At a time when thousands were dying in the
trenches and the German Command was scoffing at
Britain's 'contemptible little army', the critic said he
suddenly understood what it was all about.

The rights and wrongs of war

Many modern productions of the play have played down
its stirring patriotism. They have been more keen to show
the horrors of war, for example, by emphasizing the
killing of prisoners at Agincourt. Kenneth Branagh's
1989 film of the play dwells on the long, hard march to
Calais and on the exhausting and bloody Battle of
Agincourt. Branagh stresses the pointlessness of war and
the waste of human life.

In the mid-1980s, another director likened the play to
the Falklands War. He saw in it an unnecessary display of
power. For him, Henry was a cold man with a will of
iron, who ruthlessly manipulated people. The English
troops were also depicted in this production as bigoted
football hooligans invading the Continent. Many people
were offended by this view of the play. 'I was ashamed to
be English,' said one member of the audience. Others
agreed that the director was wrong to play down Henry's
humanity and bravery, because that was not what
Shakespeare intended. But by presenting him as hard
and unfeeling, the director was making clear his view
about the 'wrongness' of the Falklands War. Was he right,
though, to use Shakespeare's play to do so?

*In this scene from the play
(Act 5, Scene 2), taken from
a 19th-century illustrated
edition of Shakespeare's
works, Henry woos
Katherine, the daughter of
the king of France.*

12

The story of Henry V

Before the play begins, an actor (Chorus) appears on the stage. With fulsome words, he compares Henry V to Mars, the Roman god of war, ready to use his sword against his enemies.

Then Chorus changes his tone, and talks about how difficult it is to present grand scenes and action in the theatre. He asks the audience to pardon the actors for their inadequacies in bringing this great story to life. He reminds them that they are in a small 'wooden O', made by the circular walls of the playhouse. 'Can this cockpit hold The vasty fields of France?' he asks.

Using your imagination

Chorus urges the audience to use their imagination in picturing the scenes about to be acted. He asks them to imagine 1000 soldiers for each person on stage, and describes two great monarchies set against each other on either side of the Channel. He then begins to urge his listeners to become involved in the action.

He asks them to see horses, even though there are none on stage. And he reminds them that the events of many years are condensed in the play.

Imaginary forces
Think when we talk of horses that you see them
Printing their proud hooves i'th'receiving earth,
For 'tis your thoughts that now must deck our kings,
Carry them here and there, jumping o'er times,
Turning th'accomplishment of many years
Into an hour glass.

Act I Prologue

Chorus then asks the audience again for their patience, and begs them 'Gently to hear, kindly to judge our play.' He leaves the stage and *Henry V* begins.

A problem for the Church

The Archbishop of Canterbury is worried that a bill now before Parliament will deprive the Church of much of the wealth that people have donated over the years. He talks the problem over with the Bishop of Ely. Both men are very impressed by the new king. They agree that, despite his wild youth, Henry has taken on the responsibilities of kingship and become an ideal ruler.

Instead of taxing the Church, the Archbishop believes that there is another way to solve the government's money problems. He knows of an obscure law by which King Henry can lay claim to the French throne. In a meeting with Henry and his lords, he explains at length how this can be done.

Henry is uneasy. He knows that many lives will be lost. He asks the Archbishop if it is right to declare war on France. He wants to make sure that the cause is just. He is also worried that the Scots might attack England when the armed forces are abroad.

The king declares war

The king is soon convinced that war is justified. He sends for the French ambassadors. They come bearing an insulting gift of tennis balls from the Dauphin, the son of the French king. The gift is meant to imply that Henry should stick to games, not wars. War is declared and the English now start preparations to invade France.

News of Falstaff

In London, Sir John Falstaff is ill. He was Henry's companion in his wild youth. Their old cronies are upset. 'The king has killed his heart,' says Mistress Quickly, a tavern hostess and particular friend, who is at Falstaff's bedside when he dies. She describes his last moments to

The death of Falstaff

A parted e'en just between twelve and one, e'en at the turning o'the tide, for after I saw him fumble with the sheets, and play with flowers, and smile upon his finger's end, I knew there was but one way. For his nose was as sharp as a pen, and a babbled of green fields . . . a bade me lay more clothes on his feet. I put my hand into the bed, and felt them, and they were as cold as any stone.

Act II Sc iii

his friends. They grieve for him and remember incidents in his life.

Unmasking the traitors

Meanwhile, Henry has received news of three trusted noblemen, who have plotted against him and are in the pay of France. He confronts them and accuses them of treachery. They confess their guilt and beg for mercy. Henry reproaches them for their betrayal of his love and trust. In particular, he is deeply hurt by the treachery of Lord Scroop. 'Why, so didst thou?' Henry asks. 'I will weep for thee, For this revolt of thine, methinks, is like Another fall of man.' He then condemns the three to death.

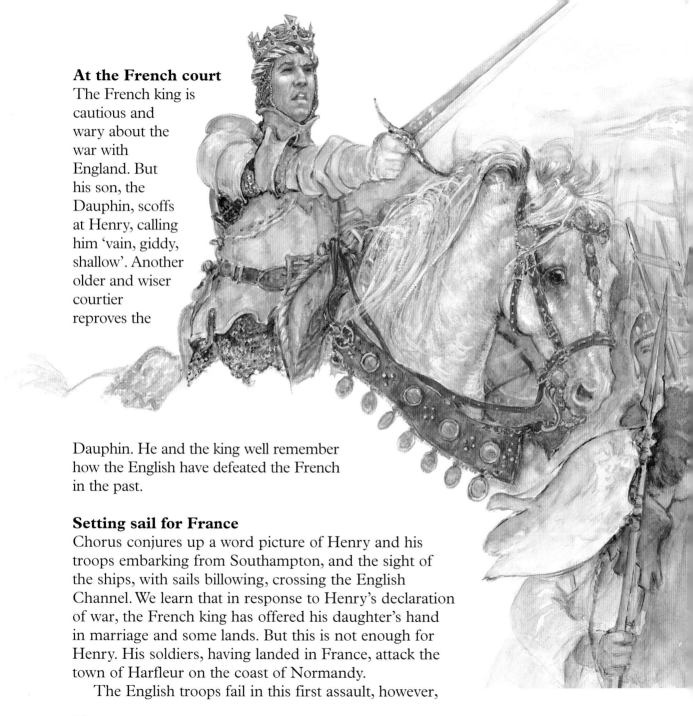

At the French court

The French king is cautious and wary about the war with England. But his son, the Dauphin, scoffs at Henry, calling him 'vain, giddy, shallow'. Another older and wiser courtier reproves the Dauphin. He and the king well remember how the English have defeated the French in the past.

Setting sail for France

Chorus conjures up a word picture of Henry and his troops embarking from Southampton, and the sight of the ships, with sails billowing, crossing the English Channel. We learn that in response to Henry's declaration of war, the French king has offered his daughter's hand in marriage and some lands. But this is not enough for Henry. His soldiers, having landed in France, attack the town of Harfleur on the coast of Normandy.

The English troops fail in this first assault, however,

and are forced to retreat. But the king urges them to make one more attack. In a stirring speech, he calls on their loyalty, patriotism and sense of honour.

Henry's rallying cry to his soldiers

Once more unto the breach, dear friends, once more,
Or close the wall up with our English dead!
In peace there's nothing so becomes a man
As modest stillness and humility.
But when the blast of war blows in our ears,
Then imitate the action of a tiger:
Stiffen the sinews, conjure up the blood,
Disguise fair nature with hard-favour'd rage . . .
Now set the teeth and stretch the nostril wide,
Hold hard the breath, and bend up every spirit
To his full height. On, on, you noble English . . .
I see you stand like greyhounds in the slips,
Straining upon the start. The game's afoot.
Follow your spirit, and upon this charge
Cry 'God for Harry, England and Saint George!'

Act III Sc i

The common soldiers

Falstaff's tavern cronies, Nym, Bardolph and Pistol, are among the soldiers. They sing to keep up their spirits on the battlefield but are urged on to fight by Llewellyn, a Welsh captain. The Boy, one of Falstaff's friends, reflects on what they really are – cowards and thieves.

Llewellyn joins two other officers, a Scot and an Englishman. They taunt each other, but avoid a full-blown quarrel when they are called back to the battlefield.

This time Harfleur's defences are broken, and Henry demands the surrender of the town. He tells the French troops and citizens that they will be slaughtered if they do not give in. The governor of the town surrenders, so Henry tells his commander to 'use mercy to them all'.

Meanwhile, in the French court, the king's daughter Katherine has her first, rather shaky, lessons in English.

Dismay at the French court

News of the English victory at Harfleur has reached the French king. His nobles cannot believe that the English have become such a fighting force. They are merely a 'barbarous people' who live in a terrible climate.

The barbarous English
Dieu de batailles, *where have they found this mettle?*
Is not their climate foggy, raw and dull,
On whom, as in despite, the sun looks pale,
Killing their fruit with frowns? Can sodden water,
A drench for sur-reined jades, their barley-broth,
Decoct their cold blood to such valiant heat?

Act III Sc vi

The king urges his nobles to make greater efforts to defeat the English, and to show how superior the French are in birth, breeding and warfare. The nobles are confident that their skill and greater numbers will win the day for France.

Trouble in the English ranks

The petty thief Bardolph has been caught stealing from the French. Llewellyn is unmoved by the pleas for mercy from his friend Pistol. The captain declares that the disciplines of war must be upheld, and that Bardolph must be condemned to death. Henry is also unrelenting. He firmly believes that conquered people should not be ill-treated and that their goods and property should not be

looted by the invading army. People benefit by treating defeated enemies kindly, he declares.

How to treat defeated enemies

. . . we give express charge that in our marches through the country there be nothing compelled from the villages, nothing taken but paid for, none of the French upbraided or abused in disdainful language. For when lenity and cruelty play for a kingdom, the gentler gamester is the soonest winner.

Act III Sc vii

In the French camp

The French nobles are anxious for the battle with the English to begin. As they wait through the long night for dawn, they boast and joke about their superior armour and horses. They are confident of winning, and are scornful of the English troops, whom they think are exhausted.

In the English camp

Chorus asks the audience to move, in imagination, from the French tents to the English troops huddled around their camp fires. There is a faint noise of activity as final preparations are made for the coming battle. The soldiers sit patiently, and inwardly worry about the dangers they will face the following morning. They are hollow-cheeked and weary, but they can see the figure of the king moving among them, giving comfort and hope to the men.

We learn that the name of the battlefield is Agincourt. (This is located northeast of Harfleur and a small distance to the south of Calais.)

Henry offers comfort to his troops

Although Henry admits to his lords that the English are in great danger, he sets out in disguise to do the rounds

of the camp. The first person he encounters is Pistol, who tries to pretend that he is an officer. Pistol also issues a threat to the Welshman Llewellyn.

Henry then meets three common soldiers. They ask whether the war with France is for a good cause, and argue that the king will pay a heavy price if it is not.

War for a good cause?

... if the cause be not good the king himself hath a heavy reckoning to make, when all those legs and arms and heads chopped off in a battle shall join together at the latter day and cry all 'We died at such a place', some swearing, some crying for a surgeon, some upon their wives left poor behind them, some upon the debts they owe, some upon their children rawly left. I am afeard there are few die well that die in battle, for how can they charitably dispose of anything when blood is their argument?

Act IV Sc i

Henry replies that the king is like every other human being. The soldiers are not convinced. They place the responsibility for the war, and the salvation or damnation of those who die in battle, on the king. Henry replies that the king is not responsible for his subjects' souls. The soldiers go on their way, with Henry agreeing to take up the quarrel with Williams, one of the men, in the future.

Burdens of kingship

As the soldiers depart, Henry reflects on the lonely burden that a king must bear in contrast to that of ordinary men. A king's life is filled with worthless flattery and empty ceremony. Henry then reveals his own fears and remorse. He owes his crown to the murder of Richard II by his father Henry IV, and fears that this might lose him God's favour – and the battle.

> ### The uselessness of ceremony
> *We must bear all.*
> *O hard condition, twin-born of greatness,*
> *Subject to the breath of every fool, whose sense*
> *No more can feel but his own wringing.*
> *What infinite heart's ease must kings neglect*
> *That private men enjoy?*
> *And what have kings that privates have not too,*
> *Save ceremony, save general ceremony?*
> *And what art thou, thou idol ceremony?*
>
> Act IV Sc i

Before the battle

The French nobles anticipate an easy victory. They mock the English army in their ragged clothes, and hurry away impatiently to the battlefield.

The English lords, however, are apprehensive about the battle which is about to begin. They know that their troops are heavily outnumbered, but they are courageous men. If they do not meet again, they will meet in heaven, says one of them.

When the king appears, one of his commanders expresses the wish that they had more men. But Henry disagrees. If they are to lose the battle, he would not want to waste more English lives.

> ### Fearful odds
> *If we are mark'd to die, we are enough*
> *To do our country loss. And if to live,*
> *The fewer men, the greater share of honour.*
> *God's will, I pray thee wish not one man more.*
>
> Act IV Sc iii

The king orders one of his lords to read a proclamation, allowing any soldier to leave before the battle. He will be given a passport and money to return home, if he chooses to do so. Henry then delivers a rousing, patriotic speech, declaring that he will share fame and brotherhood with those – the 'few' – who fight with him on this St Crispian's Day.

The Feast of Crispian
This day is called the Feast of Crispian.
He that outlives this day and comes home safe
Will stand a-tiptoe when this day is nam'd,
And rouse him at the name of Crispian.
He that shall live this day and see old age
Will yearly on the vigil feast his neighbours,
And say 'Tomorrow is Saint Crispian.'
Then he will strip his sleeve and show his scars,
And say, 'These wounds I had on Crispin's day.'
Old men forget, yet all shall be forgot
But he'll remember, with advantages,
What feats he did that day . . .
This story shall the good man teach his son,
And Crispin Crispian shall ne'er go by
From this day to the ending of the world
But we in it shall be remembered.
We few, we happy few, we band of brothers –
For he today that sheds his blood with me
Shall be my brother; be he ne'er so vile
This day shall gentle his condition –
And gentlemen in England, now abed,
Shall think themselves accurs'd they were not here,
And hold their manhoods cheap whiles any speaks
That fought with us upon Saint Crispin's Day.

Act IV Sc iii

23

A French herald arrives and asks Henry to agree to a ransom and thus save his men. The king refuses, saying that although his troops look dishevelled they will fight bravely. And so the battle begins.

Confusion on the battlefield

The French attack has collapsed but the French nobles want to lead another charge. They would prefer to die honourably than live in shame.

When it appears that French reinforcements have entered the battle, Henry orders that all prisoners be killed. It seems also that the French have massacred unarmed boys who were guarding the English baggage. Henry is very angry and sends a message to the French – they must fight or flee, and all prisoners will be killed.

At that moment, the French herald arrives. He acknowledges that the English have won the battle, and asks permission to bury the dead French soldiers.

Taking up a challenge

Earlier in the play, the disguised king had agreed to take up his dispute with Williams, one of his soldiers, at a later time. As a practical joke, he sends Llewellyn to take up the challenge. He then becomes alarmed that a real fight will develop between Williams and Llewellyn and sends two lords to prevent it. Although blows have been struck, a serious quarrel is avoided. At this moment, the king appears and confesses that he was the man with whom Williams had the argument. The soldier asks his pardon and Henry, perhaps by way of an apology, fills his glove with gold coins.

Chorus now takes up the story and tells of Henry's triumphal return to London. There are several years of peace negotiations before Henry and his men return to

to sign the peace treaty. Llewellyn and Pistol are among the soldiers in the English camp.

England versus Wales
Llewellyn and Pistol have quarrelled before, but their differences now come to a head after Pistol once more insults Llewellyn's Welsh nationality. Llewellyn strikes Pistol and forces him to eat a leek, a symbol of Wales.

Llewellyn's revenge
I peseech you heartily, scurvy, lousy knave, at my desires and my requests and my petitions, to eat, look you, this leek. Pecause, look you, you do not love it, nor your affections and your appetites and your digestions does not agree with it, I would desire you to eat it . . . If you can mock a leek, you can eat a leek.

Act v Sc i

Defeated and humiliated, Pistol decides that he will return to England and take up a life of petty crime. He will pretend that the scars from Llewellyn's beating are the result of war wounds.

Peace settlements
The French king and his nobles meet Henry and his lords in a French palace. The Duke of Burgundy makes an eloquent plea for peace. He describes the devastation of the countryside caused by the fighting, and how men become uncivilized and 'grow like savages' when a nation is at war. Henry replies that peace depends on the French agreeing to his conditions. His lords leave to draw up contracts and settlements with the French nobles.

Henry is now left alone with Katherine, the French king's daughter, and her lady-in-waiting, Alice.

One of Henry's peace conditions is the hand of Princess Katherine in marriage. This means that his heirs (rather than himself, as he had demanded earlier) will inherit the French throne.

Language difficulties

He now sets out to woo the princess – somewhat awkwardly since neither speaks the other's language. The princess is confused and does not know what to think. Henry presents himself as a plain soldier. He says that he lacks the graces and airs with which a nobleman usually courts a lady.

A soldier's love

And while thou livest, dear Kate, take a fellow of plain and uncoined constancy, for he perforce must do thee right, because he hath not the gift to woo in other places. For these fellows of infinite tongue that can rhyme themselves into ladies' favours, they do always reason themselves out again. What? A speaker is but a prater, a rhyme is but a ballad, a good leg will fall, a straight back will stoop, a black beard will turn white, a curled pate will grow bald, a fair face will wither, a full eye will wax hollow – but a good heart, Kate, is the sun and the moon, or rather the sun and not the moon, for it shines bright and never changes, but keeps his course truly. If you would have such a one, take me. And take me, take a soldier. Take a soldier, take a king. And what sayest thou then to my love?

Act v Sc ii

Henry declares his love for Katherine and asks her if she will marry him. She says only if it pleases her father. When the king assures her that it does, she agrees.

Henry then attempts to kiss her hand but she protests. He then says he will kiss her on the lips, but Katherine is

shocked. This is not the custom in France, she declares. But Henry tells her that 'nice customs curtsy to great kings . . . We are the makers of manners'. He kisses her just as the French king and various courtiers arrive.

Marriage preparations
They confirm that all the agreements have been reached and France and England are now at peace. Henry acknowledges the princess as his future queen and, after a blessing is bestowed on the marriage by Katherine's mother, preparations for the wedding are announced. Chorus comes on to the stage and ends the play, foretelling the birth of the future Henry VI.

The play's characters

Henry V

Henry V

The young king is a more complex person than he at first appears. There are many instances throughout the play where he shows himself to be the model king. His dignity stands out by comparison with the boastful, vain and foolish French. At Agincourt, he shares the anxieties of the common soldiers but his genuine courage and heroism inspire them to victory. He is also a thoughtful and devout man. At the beginning of the play, he worries about the terrible consequences of war, and when the battle is won he praises God, not himself, for the victory. Yet we can also see a devious and manipulative side to his character. The churchmen urge Henry to go to war in order to save church property. Does he agree because he has a liking for war, since the cause is not particularly just? He shows a coldness and cruelty not only in his treatment of his old friend Falstaff but also in his threats to the people of Harfleur. Henry's humility in wooing the

A humble king

. . . thou wouldst find me such a plain king that thou wouldst think I had sold my farm to buy my crown.

Act V Sc ii

French princess as a 'plain soldier' also strikes an uneasy note. Although he does it in a bluff and charming way, we know and he knows that the princess is already promised to him as part of the peace settlement. Henry was a great king, and Shakespeare takes great pains to point this out but he also shows some darker sides to his hero's nature. We are dubious about some of Henry's motives and actions while at the same time recognizing his heroic and monumental stature. It is Shakespeare's genius to make us aware of these contradictions.

Princess Katherine
The daughter of the French king, Katherine seems a young innocent girl and a dutiful daughter. She is instructed rather comically in English by her lady-in-waiting, but does not come across as a young woman with much personality. Although she is simply the 'love interest' in the play, her scenes add a light and often charming element to the play. Henry begins to woo her by calling her an angel, but she is dismissive of this. She is then confused as he begs for her love, and asks how she can love an enemy of France. He assures her that when they marry France will be as much hers as his – a reminder that she is his reward for victory over France. Finally, Katherine agrees to the marriage if it pleases her father.

Princess Katherine

Katherine's response to Henry
What says she, fair one? That the tongues of men are full of deceits?

Act V Sc ii

Llewellyn

Pistol

Llewellyn

A Welsh officer in the king's army, Llewellyn is somewhat humourless and pedantic. He is rather a comic character with a strong Welsh accent. Llewellyn is keen on the disciplines of war and quotes the classic battles of the ancient Romans as his model. He is full of admiration for Henry and compares him to Alexander the Great. The Welshman is also hot-tempered and exchanges sharp words with several of his fellow soldiers. He is particularly annoyed by Pistol's anti-Welsh mockery and forces him to eat a leek. Llewellyn is a brave and courageous soldier and fiercely loyal to the king. In this respect, Shakespeare possibly intended him to represent the common soldier inspired by Henry's heroic leadership.

Llewellyn's temper

For I do know Llewellyn
valiant,
And, touch'd with choler,
hot as gunpowder,
And quickly will return an
injury.

Act IV Sc vii

Pistol

Llewellyn calls Pistol a 'rascally, scald, beggarly, lousy, pragging knave'. This old friend of Falstaff's, renowned for his bragging and grandiose talk, finds himself on the battlefield in France where, typically, he tries to avoid the fighting. Later, in another typical gesture, he attempts to extract a ransom from a captured French soldier without success. 'I did never know so full a voice issue from so empty a heart,' says his interpreter. Penniless and humiliated by Llewellyn, who has made him eat a leek, Pistol remains irrepressible and, with characteristic bravado, decides to return to London and earn a living as a thief.

Pistol's character

For Pistol, he hath a killing
tongue and a quiet sword,
by the means whereof a
breaks words and keeps
whole weapons.

Act III Sc iii

The life and plays of Shakespeare

Life of Shakespeare

1564 William Shakespeare born at Stratford-upon-Avon.

1582 Shakespeare marries Anne Hathaway, eight years his senior.

1583 Shakespeare's daughter, Susanna, is born.

1585 The twins, Hamnet and Judith, are born.

1587 Shakespeare goes to London.

1591-2 Shakespeare writes *The Comedy of Errors*. He is becoming well-known as an actor and writer.

1592 Theatres closed because of plague.

1593-4 Shakespeare writes *Titus Andronicus* and *The Taming of the Shrew*: he is a member of the theatrical company, the Chamberlain's Men.

1594-5 Shakespeare writes *Romeo and Juliet*.

1595 Shakespeare writes *A Midsummer Night's Dream*.

1595-6 Shakespeare writes *Richard II*.

1596 Shakespeare's son, Hamnet, dies. Shakespeare writes *King John* and *The Merchant of Venice*.

1597 Shakespeare buys New Place in Stratford.

1597-8 Shakespeare writes *Henry IV*.

1599 Shakespeare's theatre company opens the Globe Theatre.

1599-1600 Shakespeare writes *As You Like It*, *Henry V* and *Twelfth Night*.

1600-01 Shakespeare writes *Hamlet*.

1602-03 Shakespeare writes *All's Well That Ends Well*.

1603 Elizabeth I dies. James I becomes king. Theatres closed because of plague.

1603-04 Shakespeare writes *Othello*.

1605 Theatres closed because of plague.

1605-06 Shakespeare writes *Macbeth* and *King Lear*.

1606-07 Shakespeare writes *Antony and Cleopatra*.

1607 Susanna Shakespeare marries Dr John Hall. Theatres closed because of plague.

1608 Shakespeare's granddaughter, Elizabeth Hall, is born.

1609 *Sonnets* published. Theatres closed because of plague.

1610 Theatres closed because of plague. Shakespeare gives up his London lodgings and retires to Stratford.

1611-12 Shakespeare writes *The Tempest*.

1613 Globe Theatre burns to the ground during a performance of *Henry VIII*.

1616 Shakespeare dies on 23 April.

Shakespeare's plays

The Comedy of Errors
Love's Labour's Lost
Henry VI Part 2
Henry VI Part 3
Henry VI Part 1
Richard III
Titus Andronicus
The Taming of the Shrew
The Two Gentlemen of Verona
Romeo and Juliet
Richard II
A Midsummer Night's Dream
King John
The Merchant of Venice
Henry IV Part 1
Henry IV Part 2
Much Ado About Nothing
Henry V
Julius Caesar
As You Like It
Twelfth Night
Hamlet
The Merry Wives of Windsor
Troilus and Cressida
All's Well That Ends Well
Othello
Measure for Measure
King Lear
Macbeth
Antony and Cleopatra
Timon of Athens
Coriolanus
Pericles
Cymbeline
The Winter's Tale
The Tempest
Henry VIII

Index

Numerals in *italics* refer to picture captions.

Picture credits
p.3 Bridgeman Art Library; p.5 AKG
London; p.6 Art Archive/Victoria and
Albert Museum, London/Harper Collins
Publishers; p.7 Bridgeman Art Library;
p.11 AKG London